FUN with FOOD WEBS

I0794062

ARCTIC FOOD WEBS

Written by Charis Mather

KidHaven PUBLISHING

Published in 2024 by
KidHaven Publishing, an Imprint of Greenhaven Publishing, LLC
2544 Clinton St., Buffalo, NY 14224

Written by: Charis Mather
Edited by: Rebecca Phillips-Bartlett
Designed by: Jasmine Pointer

Image Credits
All images are courtesy of Shutterstock.com, unless otherwise specified—with thanks to Getty Images, Thinkstock Photo, and iStockphoto. Cover – murattellioglu, evaurban, Olga Maksimava, Goinyk Production, Tory Kallman. 4–5 – Christopher Wood, Sophia Granchinho. 6–7 – Trismegist san. 8–9 – Serg Zastavkin, Ivanova Viktoriya. 10–11 – Rattiya Thongdumhy, ssawpics. 12–13 – Risto Raunio, Sergey Krasnoshchokov, Jim Cumming, Alexey Seafarer, RLS Photo, Rvector, In-Finity. 14–15 – Shawn Harper. Credit: Hidden Ocean 2005 Expedition: NOAA Office of Ocean Exploration. Public domain, via Wikimedia Commons, Totti, CC BY-SA 4.0 <https://creativecommons.org/licenses/by-sa/4.0>, via Wikimedia Commons. 16–17 – Dolores M. Harvey, Marius Ciornii. 18–19 – vladsilver, Martin Prochazkacz, Agami Photo Agency. 20–21 – Sylvie Bouchard, Himanshu Saraf. 22–23 – Petr Simon, Yuriy Kulik, United States. National Marine Fisheries Service. Public domain, via Wikimedia Commons, B. Sheiko, Public domain, via Wikimedia Commons, NOAA FishWatch, Public domain, via Wikimedia Commons, The Hidden Ocean, Arctic 2005 Exploration, NOAA-OE, Public domain, via Wikimedia Commons.

Cataloging-in-Publication Data

Names: Mather, Charis, 1999-.
Title: Arctic food webs / Charis Mather.
Description: Buffalo, New York: KidHaven Publishing, 2024. |
Series: Fun with food webs | Includes glossary and index.
Identifiers: ISBN 9781534545960 (pbk.) | ISBN 9781534545977 (library bound) |
ISBN 9781534545984 (ebook)
Subjects: LCSH: Tundra ecology--Arctic regions--Juvenile literature. |
Food chains (Ecology)--Arctic regions--Juvenile literature.
Classification: LCC QH541.5.T8 M38 2024 | DDC 577.5'8609113--dc23

Manufactured in the United States of America

CPSIA compliance information: Batch #CW24KH: For further information contact Greenhaven Publishing LLC at 1-844-317-7404.

Please visit our website, www.greenhavenpublishing.com.
For a free color catalog of all our high-quality books, call toll free 1-844-317-7404 or fax 1-844-317-7405.

Find us on

CONTENTS

Words that look like ***THIS*** can be found in the glossary on page 24.

The Arctic Ecosystem

The Arctic is very cold and covered in ice—but it is also full of life! This freezing **environment**, together with all the plants and animals that live there, makes up the Arctic **ecosystem**.

When it comes to food, each living thing in the Arctic ecosystem has an important part to play. Not many plants can grow here, so many animals eat other animals to survive, or stay alive.

Food Chains and Food Webs

Food chains show the order in which living things are eaten. Those that make their own food are at the bottom. The most dangerous diners are at the top.

an Arctic food chain

If living things eat or are eaten by many other living things, they can be part of many different food chains. When there are many connections between food chains, this makes a food web.

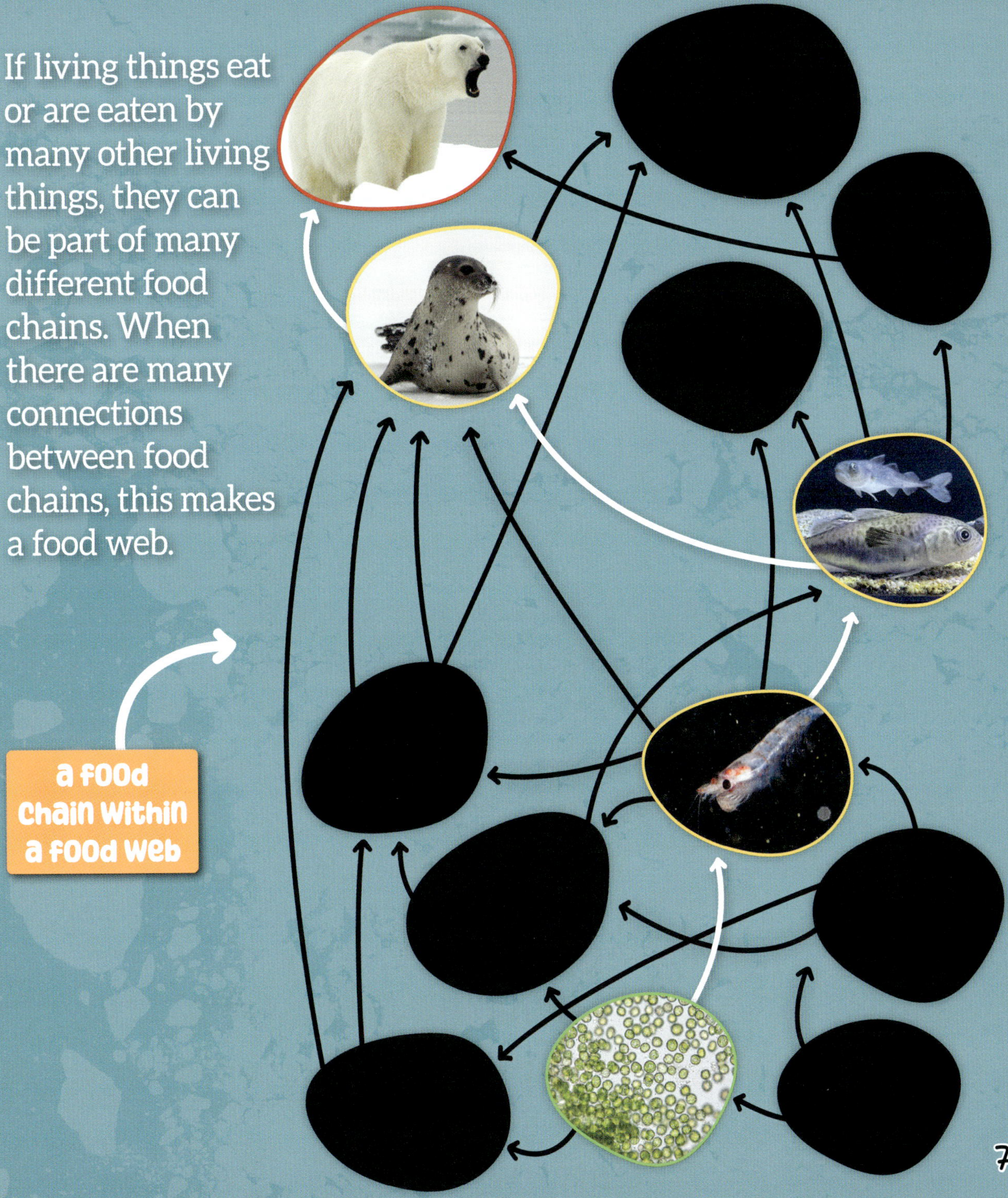

PRODUCERS

The bottom of a food web is made up of producers. Most make their own food with the help of sunlight. Producers do not need to eat other living things.

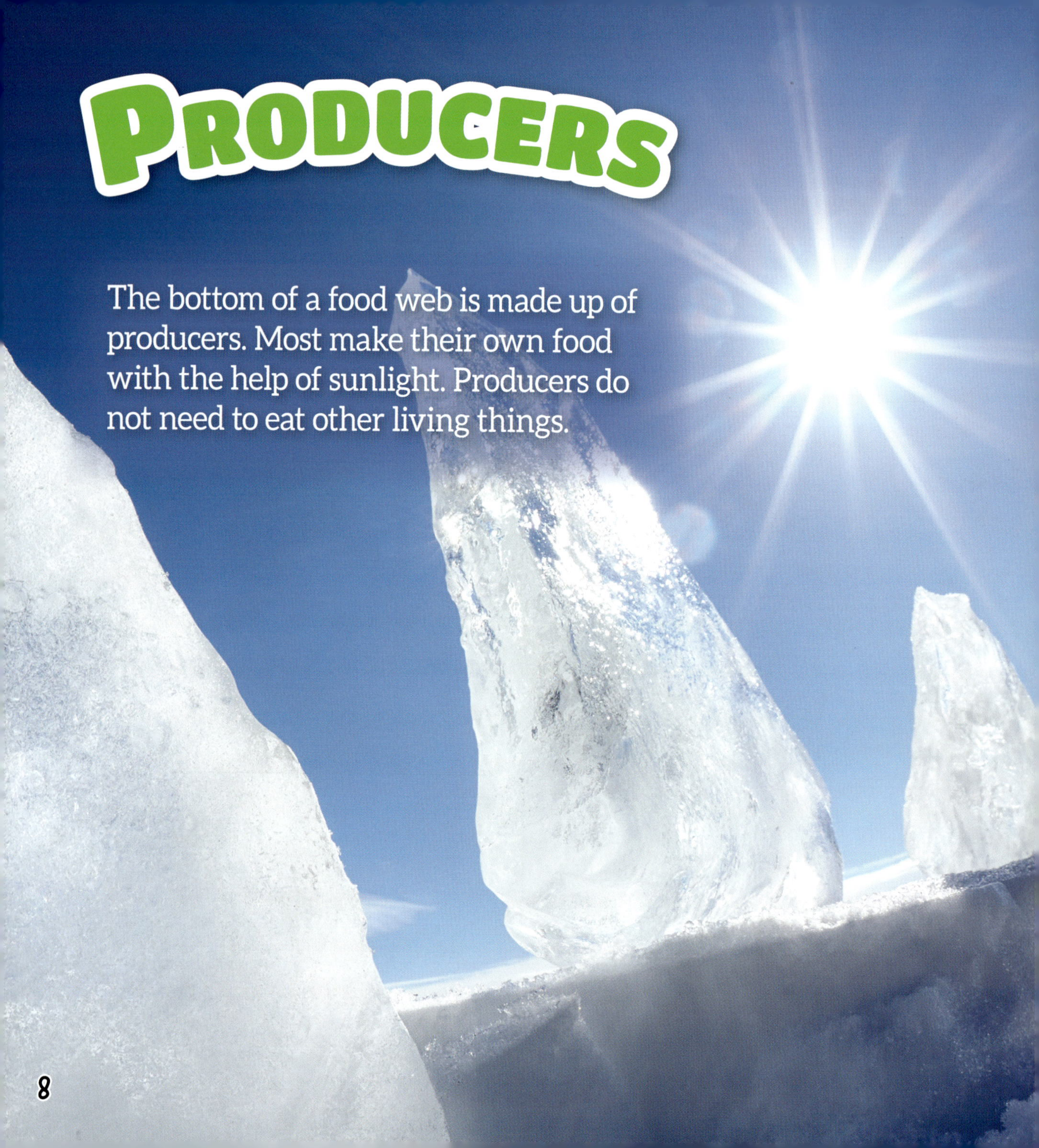

What producers live near you?

Animals that eat producers often need to eat a lot of them to get all the **ENERGY** they need. Plants are the most common producers, but not all producers are plants.

Phytoplankton

Food:
Sunlight helps them make their own food.

Eaten by:
krill, small fish, shrimp

Zoomed-in picture of phytoplankton

Phytoplankton are the main producers in the Arctic. Huge numbers of these tiny living things can be found in the icy waters, but they are too small to see with the naked eye.

ALGAE

Algae are another kind of Arctic producer. Algae can be found growing under sea ice.

Food:	**Eaten by:**
Sunlight helps them make their own food.	krill, small fish, shrimp

These Arctic producers stay near the top of the water so they get enough sunlight.

Consumers

Consumers are living things that eat other living things. Some consumers, called herbivores, only eat plants. Carnivores eat meat. Omnivores eat plants and meat.

Krill

Food:
phytoplankton, algae

Eaten by:
Arctic cod, seals, whales, squid, shrimp

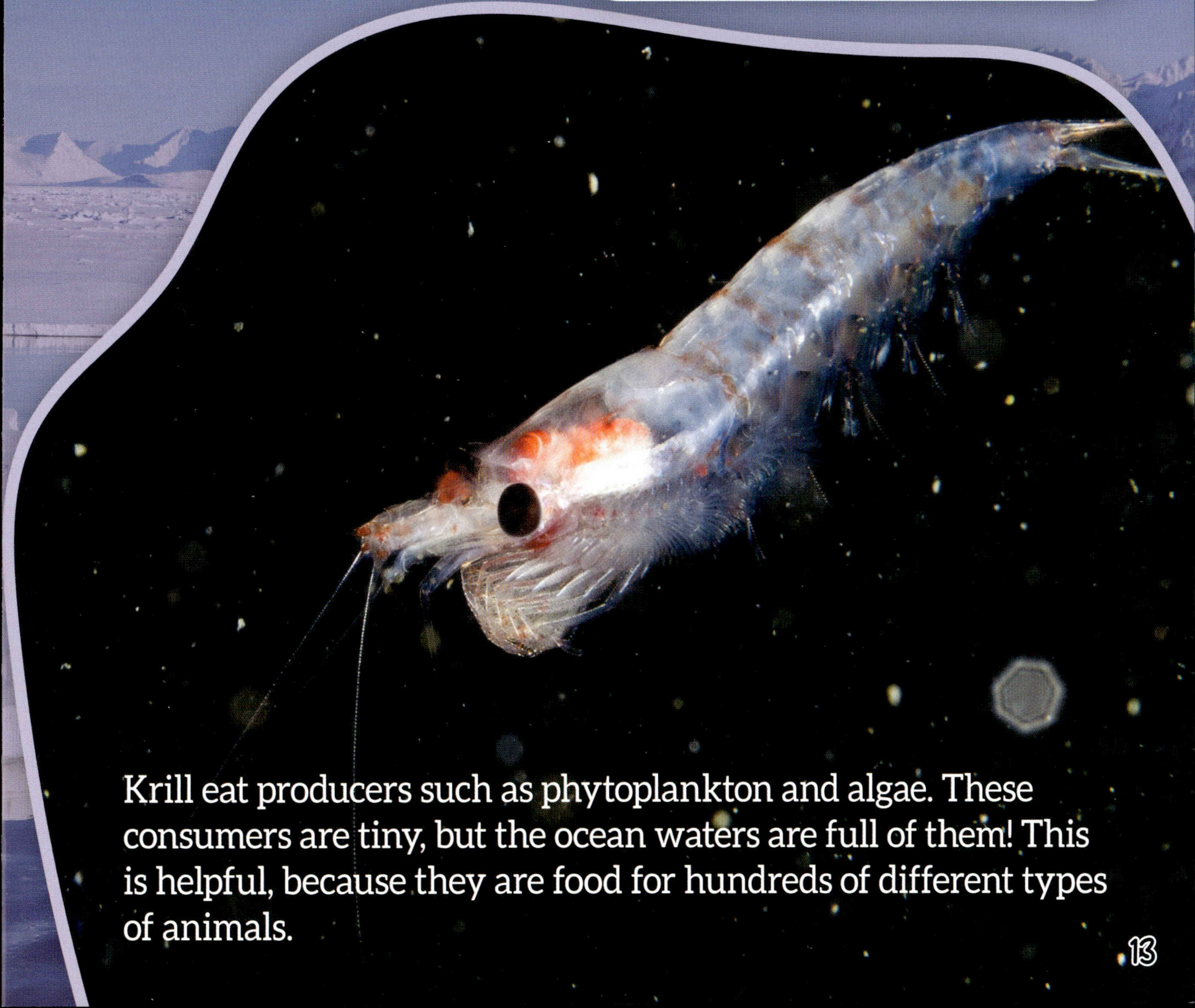

Krill eat producers such as phytoplankton and algae. These consumers are tiny, but the ocean waters are full of them! This is helpful, because they are food for hundreds of different types of animals.

Arctic Cod

While many fish would freeze in the cold Arctic waters, Arctic cod do not. These fish have special blood that stops them from freezing. This makes them a very important part of their ecosystem.

Food: krill, shrimp

Eaten by: seals, whales, birds, orcas

These consumers eat krill, shrimp, and other small animals in the ocean. They are food for many different animals in the Arctic food web, such as seals, whales, and birds.

Seals

Seals are carnivores. For many seals, fish like Arctic cod are their main **source** of food. However, that does not stop seals from going after smaller **prey**, such as krill.

Food: fish, shrimp, squid, krill

Eaten by: polar bears, orcas

Seals are covered in a thick layer of fat, called blubber. While this helps seals survive in the cold water as they hunt, it also makes them a tasty treat for orcas and polar bears.

Apex Predators

Apex predators are consumers that are not eaten by any other creature in their ***NATURAL*** environment. This puts them at the top of food webs.

What do you think a creature needs to be an apex predator?

ORCAS

FOOD: fish, squid, seals

EATEN BY: no one

Orcas are one of the top apex predators in oceans all around the world. As Arctic ice melts, orcas travel farther north and become another threat to smaller Arctic animals.

Polar Bears

Polar bears are apex predators on the ice, but they are such excellent swimmers that prey is not even safe in the water! Their size and sharp teeth make them successful hunters.

No Arctic animals are completely safe from polar bears, but the main prey of this apex predator is the seal. Polar bears will wait to catch seals by holes in the ice.

FOOD: seals, walruses, narwhals, caribou, birds

EATEN BY: no one

An Arctic Food Web

Take a look at this food web to see how energy moves through the Arctic ecosystem. Start with the sun at the bottom and follow the arrows to see what is eaten by what.

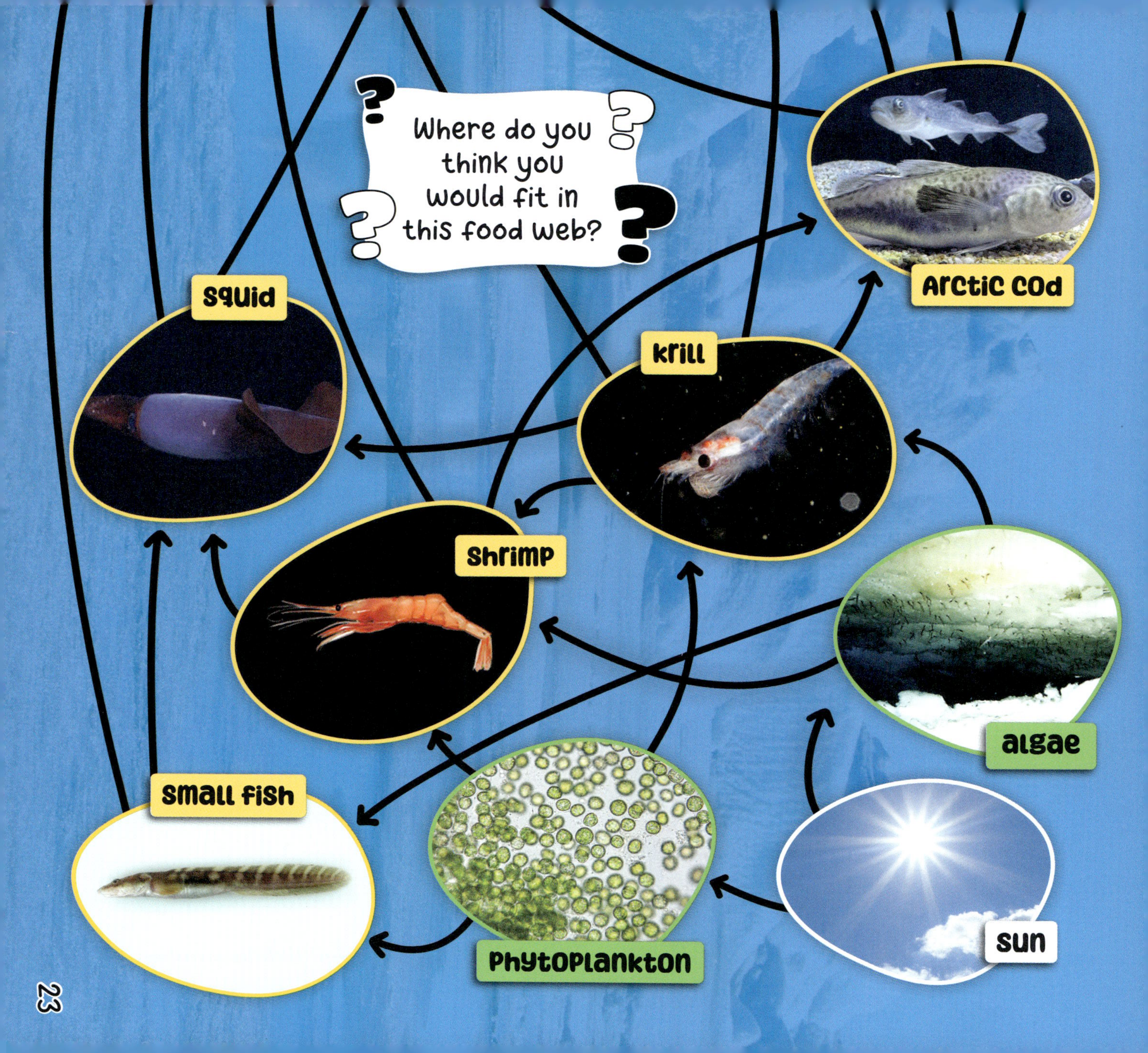
Where do you think you would fit in this food web?
Arctic cod
squid
krill
shrimp
algae
small fish
phytoplankton
sun

GLOSSARY

ecosystem a community of living things and the area they live in

energy the ability to do work

environment everything in the world not made by people

natural having to do with the parts of the world not made by people

predators animals that hunt other animals for food

prey animals that are hunted by other animals for food

source where something comes from

INDEX